ILLUSTRATOR'S
REFERENCE
MANUAL
CHILDREN

ILLUSTRATOR'S
REFERENCE
MANUAL
CHILDREN

CHARTWELL
BOOKS, INC.

A QUARTO BOOK

Published by Chartwell Books
A Division of Book Sales, Inc.
110 Enterprise Avenue
Secaucus, New Jersey 07094

ISBN 1 55521 565 3

This book was designed and produced by
Quarto Publishing plc
The Old Brewery, 6 Blundell Street
London N7 9BH

Photographer: Peter Hince
Assistant: Anjuli Raychaudhuri
Stylist: Tony Williams
Designer: Karin Skånberg
Assistant art director: Chlöe Alexander
Editor: Kate Kirby
Art directors: Moira Clinch, Nick Buzzard
Editorial director: Carolyn King

Typeset by QV Typesetting, London
Manufactured in Hong Kong by Regent Publishing Services
Limited
Printed by Lee Fung Asco Printers Limited

Contents

0-18 months

1·01   Mother holding baby
1·02   Nursing
1·03   Bubbling baby
1·04   Carried in a baby sling
1·05   Bathtime
1·06   Diaper changing
1·07   Drying baby
1·08   Being dressed
1·09   Up in the air
1·10   A bottlefeeding from daddy
1·11   Wrapped in a shawl
1·12   Having a snooze
1·13   Lying on back crying
1·14   Lying on stomach laughing
1·15   Lying in carriage
1·16   On the potty
1·17   Sitting in diaper
1·18   Taking teddy for a trip
1·19   First steps
1·20   Playing the tambourine
1·21   Standing in winter clothes
1·22   Playing with toy aeroplane
1·23   Figuring it out
1·24   A game before bedtime
1·25   Riding a rocking horse
1·26   Sitting in highchair
1·27   A ride in a stroller
1·28   Comforting baby sister
1·29   Family group

18 months-3 years

2·01 Enjoying a treat
2·02 Having a drink
2·03 Looking at picture books
2·04 Teddy bear's picnic
2·05 What's in the toybox?
2·06 A box of surprises
2·07 Enjoying a book
2·08 Hello, goodby!
2·09 Out in the rain
2·10 Roughhousing
2·11 Playing with mum

3-5 years

3·01 Time for a story
3·02 "Giant's footsteps"
3·03 Sucking thumb
3·04 Having a snack
3·05 Going swimming
3·06 Building a sandcastle
3·07 A new pair of water wings
3·08 Playing catch
3·09 Riding a tricycle
3·10 Making funny faces
3·11 Dressing up
3·12 Spiderman – to the rescue!
3·13 Hopping
3·14 Tightrope walking
3·15 Painting a picture
3·16 Playing with toy bus
3·17 Combing doll's hair
3·18 Boy and his dog
3·19 On adult's shoulders
3·20 Carrying a huge cushion
3·21 Ready for bed
3·22 Bedtime story

5-10 years

4·01 Pulling on trousers
4·02 Putting on boots
4·03 Pulling on boots
4·04 Putting on winter coat
4·05 After school play
4·06 Anyone for tennis?
4·07 The ballet lesson
4·08 With plane . . .
4·09 . . . Ready for takeoff
4·10 Time for a snack
4·11 Folding clothes
4·12 Perched on high chair
4·13 Playing with construction toy
4·14 Playing with dollhouse
4·15 Playing with model car
4·16 Lying reading comic
4·17 Sitting reading comic
4·18 Sitting on bike
4·19 To the beach
4·20 Diving
4·21 Head over heels
4·22 Doing a handstand
4·23 Little monster!
4·24 Saying prayers

10-15 years

5·01 Doing up school tie
5·02 Opening schoolbag
5·03 Off to school
5·04 Playing cricket
5·05 Doing homework
5·06 Lacing up sneakers
5·07 Rollerskating
5·08 Riding on skateboard
5·09 Bike repairs
5·10 Getting on bike
5·11 Riding bike
5·12 Playing guitar
5·13 At the beach
5·14 Flipping through teen magazine
5·15 On the telephone
5·16 What to wear?
5·17 Putting on make up
5·18 Fixing hair
5·19 The chess game
5·20 Holding hands
5·21 Peck on cheek

Using the children manual

Overhead
camera angle

Waist-level
camera angle

Floor-level
camera angle

The ILLUSTRATOR'S REFERENCE MANUAL: CHILDREN comprises 112 poses categorized under five headings based on age of subject. Each category has a code number, and within each category each pose has a further subcode number for ease of reference.

Each pose is presented from 24 angles. The images are as large as the pose will conveniently allow. Consequently, although a consistent scale is maintained within the camera angles on each page, the scale changes from one page to another within the same pose. In order to facilitate the drawing of group illustrations, a simple calibrated bar accompanies each set of camera angles which are to the same scale. To draw a pose combining two or more figures, use a camera lucida to enlarge or reduce the calibrated bar on chosen angles until a precise match is obtained. This will ensure that the figures are all drawn to the same scale.

Each pose is presented from 24 angles, achieved by using three cameras, and a turntable rotated through 360° (above). A simple camera angle symbol (above left) accompanies the relevant group of images within a pose.

Overhead
camera angle

Waist-level
camera angle

Floor-level
camera angle

Pose A   Pose B   Pose C

A

B

C

Composite figures (above) can be drawn using elements from different poses. The calibrated bar allows elements from poses presented in different scales to be combined.

Group illustrations (below) can easily be drawn. The calibrated bar accompanying each pose can be used to standardize the scales.

REFERENCE MANUAL CHILDREN

1·29

0–18 MONTHS

Family group

Index and sub-index code

Category heading

Pose title

Calibrated bar

1·01 Mother holding baby

Mother holding baby

1·02 Nursing

Nursing

1·03 Bubbling baby

1·04

Carried in a baby sling

Carried in a baby sling

1·05 Bathtime

1·06 Diaper changing

Diaper changing

1·07

Drying baby

Drying baby

1·08

Being dressed

Being dressed

ILLUSTRATOR'S REFERENCE MANUAL: CHILDREN

1·09

Up in the air

1·10   A bottlefeeding from daddy

A bottlefeeding from daddy

1·11 Wrapped in a shawl

Wrapped in a shawl

1·12 Having a snooze

Having a snooze

1·13

Lying on back crying

Lying on back crying

1·14

Lying on stomach laughing

Lying on stomach laughing

1·15 Lying in carriage

Lying in carriage

1·16 On the potty

1·18

Taking teddy for a trip

Taking teddy for a trip

1·19

First steps

First steps

1·20 Playing the tambourine

Standing in winter clothes

1·22 Playing with toy plane

1·24

A game before bedtime

A game before bedtime

1·25 Riding a rocking horse

Riding a rocking horse

1·26

Sitting in highchair

Sitting in highchair

1·27

A ride in a stroller

Comforting baby sister

Comforting baby sister

ILLUSTRATOR'S REFERENCE MANUAL: CHILDREN

1·29 Family group

2·01 Enjoying a treat

Having a drink

2·03 Looking at picture books

Looking at picture books

2·04 Teddy bear's picnic

Teddy bear's picnic

2·05

What's in the toybox?

What's in the toybox?

ILLUSTRATOR'S REFERENCE MANUAL: CHILDREN

2·06 A box of surprises

A box of surprises

2·07

Enjoying a book

Enjoying a book

2·08

Hello, goodby!

Out in the rain

2·10 **Roughhousing**

Roughhousing

2·11

Playing with mum

Time for a story

"Giant's footsteps"

3·03 Sucking thumb

Having a snack

Going swimming

Building a sandcastle

A new pair of water wings

Riding a tricycle

3·10 Making funny faces

ILLUSTRATOR'S REFERENCE MANUAL: CHILDREN

Spiderman – to the rescue!

Spiderman – to the rescue!

3·13 Hopping

Tightrope walking

3·15

Painting a picture

Playing with toy bus

3·18 Boy and his dog

On adult's shoulders

On adult's shoulders

3.20 Carrying a huge cushion

3·22 Bedtime story

Pulling on trousers

Pulling on trousers

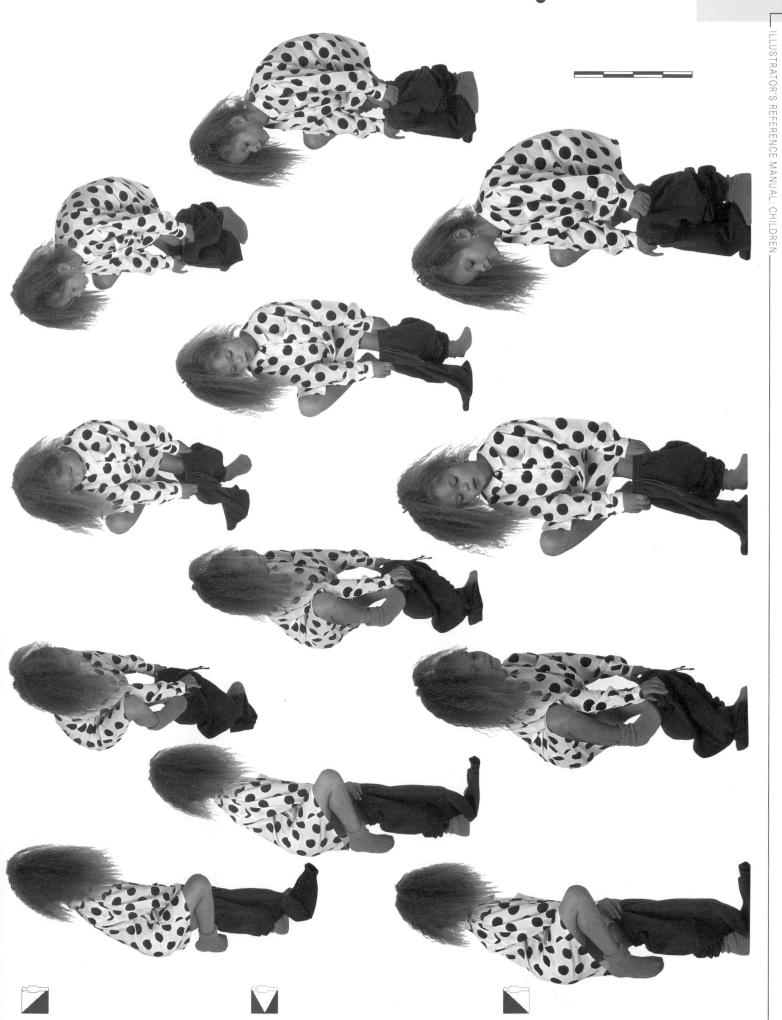

4·02

Putting on boots

Pulling on boots

4·04 Putting on winter coat

4·06 Anyone for tennis?

The ballet lesson

4·08

With plane . . .

. . . Ready for takeoff

4·10 Time for a snack

ILLUSTRATOR'S REFERENCE MANUAL: CHILDREN

4·12 Perched on high chair

Perched on high chair

4·13

Playing with construction toy

Playing with construction toy

Playing with dollhouse

4·15 Playing with model car

4·17

Sitting reading comic

4·18

Sitting on bike

4·19

To the beach

4·21 Head over heels

Doing a handstand

4·23 Little monster!

Saying prayers

5·01 Doing up school tie

Opening schoolbag

5·03 Off to school

ILLUSTRATOR'S REFERENCE MANUAL · CHILDREN

5·05 Doing homework

Doing homework

5·06 Lacing up sneakers

5·08

Riding on skateboard

Riding on skateboard

5·09 Bike repairs

5·10

Getting on bike

Getting on bike

5·11 Riding bike

5·12 **Playing guitar**

Playing guitar

5·13

At the beach

At the beach

5·14 Flipping through teen magazine

5·15

On the telephone

On the telephone

5·16

What to wear?

5·17 Putting on make up

5·19 The chess game

The chess game

5·20

Holding hands

5·21

Peck on cheek

Peck on cheek

Credits

Quarto Publishing plc would like to thank the following for their assistance in the production of this book: Circus Circus, Mothercare and Halfords

We would also like to thank the models of the M.O.T. model agency, and with thanks to David Game and George Ajayi